Gods of Four Mile Creek

Gods of Four Mile Creek

Poems, Essays, and Photographs by Phillip Howerton

Foreword by Steve Wiegenstein

ISBN: 978-1-952232-83-1

Library of Congress Control Number: 2023946690

Cover Design by Phillip Howerton and Russell Nelson

Interior Design by Phillip Howerton

Published by:
Golden Antelope Press
715 E. McPherson
Kirksville, Missouri 63501
Phone: (660) 229-2997; (660)-349-9832
Email: ndelmoni@gmail.com; betsydelmonico@gmail.com

Grateful acknowledgement is made to the editors of the following journals in which some of these poems first appeared.

American Tanka
Appalachian Journal
Big Muddy: A Journal of the Mississippi River Valley
Cantos: A Literary and Arts Journal
Capper's Weekly
Christian Science Monitor
The Comstock Review
Elder Mountain: A Journal of Ozarks Studies
Hard Row to Hoe
The Heartland Review
Intégrité: A Faith and Learning Journal
Lucidity
The Midwest Quarterly
Modern Haiku
Ozarks Alive
The Ozarks Mountaineer
OzarksWatch
Plainsongs
Slant: A Journal of Poetry

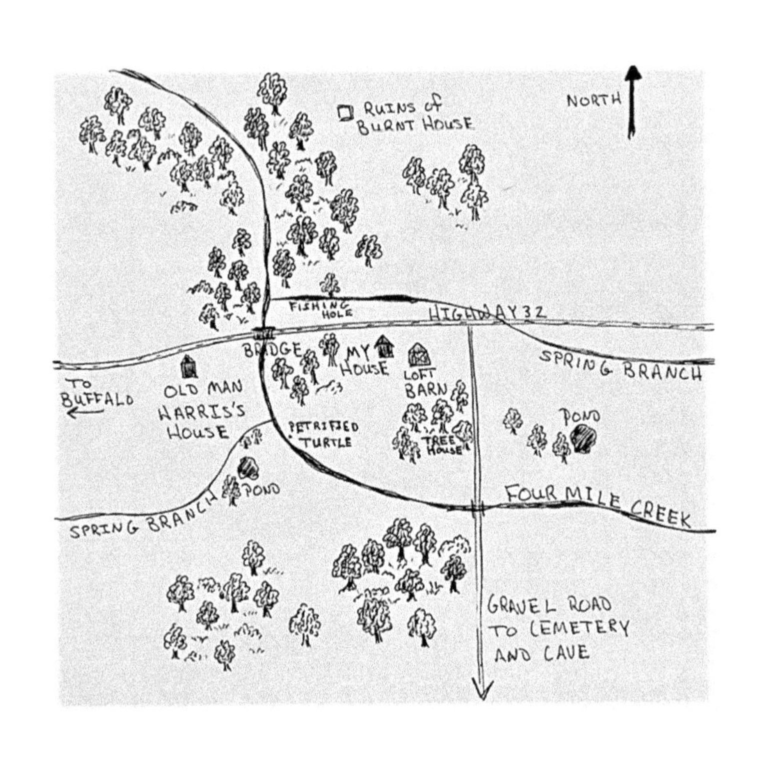
NORTH
RUINS OF BURNT HOUSE
FISHING HOLE
HIGHWAY 32
BRIDGE
MY HOUSE
LOFT BARN
SPRING BRANCH
TO BUFFALO
OLD MAN HARRIS'S HOUSE
PETRIFIED TURTLE
TREE HOUSE
POND
POND
SPRING BRANCH
FOUR MILE CREEK
GRAVEL ROAD TO CEMETERY AND CAVE

To the memory of Four Mile, Duesenberry, and Panther,
three creeks of my childhood, and to what they once were.

"Among . . . people, wherever they existed, there has always been found a religion befitting their stage of culture and clearly influenced by their geographical environment."

R. H. Whitbeck
The Influence of Geographical Environment on Religious Beliefs

"Locality gives art."

Robert Frost

". . . know the place you come from or it just might kill you."

Brian Carpenter
Introduction to *Grit Lit*

Contents

FOREWORD

What if every Ozark hollow had its own dryads and nymphs, as the Greeks imagined for their countryside, resident deities, particular spirits of the place? It's an appealing notion, one that many of us entertain when we encounter a wayside spring or a gnarled oak in the back field.

Phillip Howerton explores that idea in the opening poem of this collection, imagining what the Ozark counterparts of those mythical gods would be like, and that same merger of the down-home and the lofty inhabits the entire book. As he says in his perfectly chosen epigraph, taken from Robert Frost, "Locality gives art." These poems, essays, and photographs are deeply local, grounded in place, and yet they are also aware of broader concerns, the wider world, and the currents of history.

The reference to Frost is appropriately placed in this book, for on nearly every page I hear the ghost of Robert Frost, that great old master of the poetry of rural life in all its brutal beauty. Likewise, Howerton does not shy away from the cruelty and loss of rural existence, specifically in its Ozark manifestation. A poem like "The Google Car," for example, spoken in the voice of an elderly, visually impaired widow, balances the woman's dire situation and her instinctive resilience in a monologue that is both gentle and defiant.

It's easy to slide into mere pathos in poems dealing with aging, the loss of home or farm, or the decline of the rural economy, but Howerton avoids that pitfall with his gift for close observation. These are poems of noticing, in which small detail yields precision and impact. The emotional response comes from our recognition of a detail's perfect rightness, not from any labored effort to evoke feeling.

The photographs and essays included here, similarly, work by the sharp depiction of the specific. I'm particularly fond of the photograph accompanying "The Folklorist"; the unexpected movement within the poem, and the reframing of the narrative that unfolds in the speaker's mind as the poem progresses, make us reconsider the photograph. It is no longer an image for nostalgia or pity; or at least, not only those emotions. It is a sharp and closely observed image of a house that is at once a monument and a silent lament.

There's always pleasure in seeing traditional forms made fresh, and this collection has much to offer in that line. The fine poem "On Her Blindness" echoes not only the subject of Milton's famous sonnet on blindness, but its form as well. And many more poems explore a variety of forms.

This is not a book to be rushed through. Read a poem or two, put the book down, take a walk or a drive, and see what you notice. And if you pass a little creek or an odd-boled tree – it won't hurt to ask its blessing.

Steve Wiegenstein

Spring Flood, 1966

Summer Drought, 2022

Gods of Four Mile Creek

They sometimes tried to mimic Greek cousins
but could manage only poorest of plays,
torturing luckless crawdads and tadpoles
by withholding waters, and when raging
full froth, they would wash away water gates
or drown hay bales loitering in low fields.
They were often absent for months, and free
of them, the creek would grow calm, and water
striders glided the smooth summer surface,
autumn leaves colored the silent eddies,
or winter water gurgled beneath ice.

But they always returned to continue
ancient antics of flood and drought, pushing
gravel into bottom pastures, piling
leaves and trash in young willows, whispering
to me in morning darkness, and threatening
my footing as I waded to fetch cows.
Aloof and assured of our loyal love,
they were not jealous and needed no proof
of faith. They knew we were like the fishes
fated to fight their way upstream each spring
returning to pools that soon dried away.
Ripples could not conceal their cruel laughter—
they knew we could not resist returning,
and they believed they had nothing to give.

Folks, Dead and Living

"How enduring are our bodies after all! The forms of our brothers and sisters, our parents, children, and wives lie still in the hills and fields that surround us."

Henry David Thoreau

To Know This Place

> "Blackjack oak can withstand fire because of its thick, insulating bark and its ability to resprout. . . . [It] is a humble, unadmired tree, but we must also give credit to this rugged tree for living in places where few other trees will live."
>
> Missouri Department of Conservation

> "Sawing a dead blackjack is like carving stone."
>
> James, an Old Woodcutter

Toss aside the tourist guide, the drug and murder novel,
and the book of nostalgic poems, then go to the blackjack
in the backyard and try to shuck its bark with those tender hands
or attempt to break a limb or twig of its sinewy self.

Study the tight-lipped lobes of its leaves and their waxed
and resistant surface and bristled tips, its half and heavily hooded acorns,
hard and bead-like, which wish to be overlooked and left to roll
into an insect hole or into a crack or crevice of drought.

Study the downcast black branches hanging in tortured tangles like black-
barked lightning, and its charcoal trunk that appears to have been seared
by ancient fires, and how it doesn't deign to entertain by turning fall colors
or tossing in the wind, and note its refusal to be geometric

and its absolute contrast to the white clapboards, and try to plow the soil
it prefers with a shiny shoe heel, the red clay, chert, and sandstone.
And if you live long enough, come view it in its death; it will be little changed,
growing only harder and harder, ever more certain of what it was.

An Old Corner Post

He is ash gray, weathered, and shrunken
and has several wild hairs of wire
no one bothers to trim. Standing alone
where corners of three fields and a lawn
once met, he is no longer of use
but is too stubborn, too rooted to move.
All four lines of his people are gone,
and he probably never thought he would
outlive them all. He never offers talk,
but if you stand beside him a moment,
you will see four straight tangents
formed by scattered cedars and wild roses,
marking where fence rows once led
across fields and deep into these hills.

Peach Cobbler, 1973

Peach cobbler for dessert that Sunday.
My paternal great aunt Jewel boasted,
"Your Great-Grandmother canned
those peaches the summer she died,
twenty-one years ago." The fruit
became flesh in my mouth; I
swallowed hard, picked about the crust,
avoiding the veined, faded fruit
and cautiously pretended to be full.
Mother appeared pleased she'd refused,
but Father helped himself to seconds,
chewing in silence with eyes closed.

Wild Cherry Trees

Those Old Farmers

They loomed in distant fencerows on horizons
of my childhood. The gray of many winters
seemed always to hang heavy upon them,
and their leaden silver scales of bark
found color only from the curious greens
of lichen growing there. They did not invite
children to play near them, and their limbs
were far beyond reach, and they always held
a stern, severe stillness in their branches,
withered and broken by winds of hard times.
But when brave enough to approach alone,
I sometimes sensed a sweetness concealed
under their tight and ashen exteriors
and wondered what grief made them wish
to forget this fragrant part of themselves.

Keep Out

On each gate to his farm
he has posted a homemade warning
written in white paint
with a wide, stiff-bristled brush
on sidewalls of bald tires
or scraps of broken lumber,
and the thick letters have stringy ends,
like rags torn from his rough lexicon.
He spells the longer word differently
each time: *Trespasing*, *Trespessing*,
Trespassin, *Tresspassing*,
but folks know what he means,
and, somehow, his troubled
orthography makes the message
even more convincing.

The Last Mailbox on the Rural Route

"All changes. Families die off and others
move away, and they never come back
for their dead. My husband died early,
and I don't know anyone around here
no more. The local store closed.
The board consolidated our school
and haul the local kids like cattle
more than an hour to the county seat.
New folks have changed the names
of all the dirt roads, and my box number
has changed five times, but I've
been the last one for more than fifty years.
If I'm in my garden and hear the box
door slam at the end of the lane,
I know it's time to get some supper
and the carrier is done for the day.
I'm holding the end of the line.
I'm marking the end of something—
that's the most any of us can hope for."

On the Second Ridge North-Northeast

Travelers on the highway might see,
if they looked north-northeast
when cresting the last hill south of the bridge,
a loft barn, two ridges away, appearing
and disappearing in a parting of trees;
and they might see the black square
of emptiness left by the missing loft door,
but they would be too far away to see
the pulley and rope of the obsolete
hay lift left hanging in the loft,
and forever too far away to see
the star molded into the pulley's cover,
the star he focused upon as each load
of hay was lifted into his new barn
that he built on the second ridge
north-northeast of a little-traveled road
that he was certain went nowhere.

The Grade A Milk Barn

Unlike her older sister, the loft barn,
she will never be pretty or picturesque,
and memories will not soften her lines,
for no one shared hay-laden loft days
or manger nights with her, and she
offered no shelter from storms
nor comfort in birth or death.
She was a small factory built
of cinder blocks and concrete
with metal window frames
and store-bought door latches.
She was obsessed with cleanliness,
and her walls were always damp,
her floors wet, and the chill of extraction
was always in her touch.

Four Mile Creek

Its name is a misnomer, for it stretches
seven miles from its forked ditch beginnings
in pastures to where it glides into Niangua
River, forming a C whose ends are almost
six miles apart as a crow flies, if a crow
agrees to fly in a straight line. It first runs
west, carrying turkey litter and cow manure
on its back, crawls under Highway B
picks up some spring water, crosses two
gravel roads, and turns north to pass
under Highway 32. Sometimes flowing
above ground but often being a ghost
stream disappearing beneath its bed,
it continues north and, like a mud turtle
dislocated by drought, smells deep water
and crawls straight for the Niangua
until the rolling backside of Cowan bluff
forces it east to run parallel to the river
for a mile before it finds a low gap
and dips under Highway P, enters
a wooded marsh, and slips into the river.

Four Mile is the only concrete measure
passed down by the earliest local settlers—
the only feature to measure their measure
of experience—for there is no "100 Foot Bluff,"
no "One Mile Trail," no "Three Mile Creek,"
no "Ten Foot Stone." We often assume
that they exaggerated their past, but seven-
mile-long Four Mile Creek bears witness
that they understated, and they did so
by three-sevenths. Their summers
may have been three-sevenths hotter,
droughts three-sevenths drier, cyclones
three-sevenths deadlier, floods three-
sevenths higher, winters three-sevenths
colder, snow three-sevenths deeper, the hills
to and from school three-sevenths steeper.

They may have understated the past
knowing we would not believe, or they
were simply modest, or too proud to accept
sympathy. Maybe its name was a corruption
of the French *fourmi*, which literally means
ant and figuratively *hard worker*,
for it is a small, hardworking stream.
Perhaps, the first settler, when asked
about it replied, "This crick goes for miles."
Maybe they were being philosophical,
suggesting that this stream, like life,
is shorter than it appears, or perhaps,
like us, they tended to reduce nature,
or maybe, recollecting hardscrabble
beginnings and severity of place, didn't
want us pondering why they stopped here—
or asking why the hell they stayed.

Old Cedars

There are few places for them now,
now they are cut out of pastures,
and woods have grown thick again,
pushing them from a place in the sun.
They are no longer needed to provide green
in winter, and most of size have been logged.
Sometimes we see them at an old home place
or cemetery, pointing out where a fence line
or gate once was or standing over a grave.
We notice they have grown misshapen
during our absence, their upper branches
broken by wind and ice, and their lower
limbs, branched out of proportion,
are absently restive as if they are unsure
of how to interpret the wind or are reaching
repeatedly for something no longer there.

Porch Swing Stolen from the Old Home Place

Its straight back irritated spines and spleens,
And it was too narrow for two men to sit
And whittle nothing, spin tales, and spit,
Or for any two to shuck corn or break beans.

But its builder was twelve and used lumber
Left from the barn his silent brother built
When home from the Great War haunted by guilt.
It swung while three generations fell to slumber.

Outside a flea market that is just a "short drive,"
And has "rustic treasures and primitives,"
A man in khakis and monogrammed sleeves
Loads a "Rustic Bench" priced "$69.95."

"Why did you buy this contraption, Dear Lover?"
"To accent my flower bed—It's *so* quaint."
"But it will rot within a year, even with paint."
"C'est la vie, c'est la vie, I can always buy another."

September 15

Hershel Howerton (1935-2003)

Each year you noted summer heat would break
on or near your birthday and rains and coolness
would come. You must have noticed this when
a boy on the farm, and such awareness bred
other awareness until you could read any turn
of wind, translate notes of crickets and rain crows
and tree frogs, and foresee weather building
beyond the horizons. You have been gone
sixteen years, a parting we did not see coming,
and each day and night the wind and skies
remind me of you and remind me
that each day, regardless of the weather,
will bring joys you did not bother to predict
because you knew they would be there.

Faded Now

faded now,
the yellow towels
she bought
to brighten this place
without him

The Farm Forgets It Was a Farm

The loft barn wears the same faded sweater
every day, with elbows worn thin where boards
are missing. Brush and briars fill the garden,
and fencerows grow unruly like untrimmed
eyebrows. No one visits. Strangers glance
in as they hurry past. The doors stand open,
and the fences are down, but there is nothing
to keep in and no reason to keep anything out.
In the unmown fields, winds with no place to be
make a muffled uncertain shuffling sound,
like his stocking feet lost in his numbered hallway.

The Grandmother

She came to adulthood during the depth
of the Depression, married at eighteen,
gave birth to seven children. Suddenly
a widow, and then came a world of war,
a son killed in Korea, another
sent to Nam. “I always had my hands,”
she said, and they pulled her through the hard times
and grew thick and strong as she worked the farm,
milked her cow, raised a half-acre garden.
Then she arrived at her final winter,
to that makeshift bed in her living room—
and as a son gripped the fire poker
to tend the stove, her hands opened and closed
with an instinct to stir that bed of coals,
to build one more fire against the night.

White Oak Posts

You can still find some of these old fellows
along a fence in woods where steel posts
and wire were added. They seem obsolete,
for they long ago rotted from earth
and hang above leaf bed clinging to wire.
They were split from bottom logs of trees
during the dark of moon, dried a year,
and then driven in dark of moon.
We may laugh at such old wisdom,
but here they are, still solid at heart,
bearing witness to this boundary
and holding strands of past and present.

The Google Car
(A Widow's Complaint)

I can't see very well; macular degeneration
and the state took away my driver's license
fifty-one years ago. Sometimes people drive
up my driveway—some are neighbors
coming to buy eggs, but they always call first
because they know I can't see who they are
until they speak. Others are strangers wanting
to buy my late husband's farm equipment
in the east pasture. I know they are strangers
before they reach the house because they go
to the wrong door: neighbors go to the back door,
strangers go to the front. Others drive up
and just sit and honk or turn around
and leave, inconsiderate or lost.
One of those must have been what my
little grandson calls the Google Car.
He told me that he could drive
down the highway on his computer
in fifth grade and turn and look right up
my driveway and that this had all been filmed
by the Google Car. I don't know why
anyone would want to film my things.
If I had known that Google car was out there,
I would have gone out with my dish rag
and shooed it away. I can't do much,
and I'm embarrassed to have people
on computers gawking at my rusty mailbox,
the weeds along the driveway, or the old
loft barn blowing away with the wind—
or to see me at my kitchen window
straining eyes to see if anyone is out there.

Five Cemetery Poems

I. The Pasture Cemetery

> In many parts of the Ozark country one hears tales
> of moving lights, which usually appear in cemeteries.
> Vance Randolph
> *Ozark Magic and Folklore*

These dead chose their place of rest.
Refusing to be relegated to rocky slope,
they staked a claim in a broad pasture,
surrounding themselves with young cedars
to witness their remains. Now aged evergreens
are broken by storm, and dumb stones
are pushed athwart or face down by cattle,
but no signs from beyond signal complaint
or revenge; winds moan here unheard,
if they moan; the landowner sleeps
deeply, and neighbors live undisturbed,
for no great-grandfather rises from soil
with rotted overalls and collapsed face
muttering oaths with a mouth of fire
and ragged teeth; indeed, not even a light,
floating harmless and soft has appeared.
Perhaps these dead are practical folks,
who note that their earthly square
requires no mowing of grass, no mending
of fence and would view remembrance
by the living as mere superstition,
sentimentality, sham and nonsense,
and remain silent in acquiescence,
or perhaps they know the most potent
curse upon the living is for us
to have a past that touches us not.

II. Three Field Stones in a Hill Cemetery

Immediately inside the main gate
on the left are three field stones leading
a line of grave markers up the north slope.
Nothing is known of these stones;
church records make no mention,
and the county's cemetery census
lists these residents as "field stones."
Perhaps nothing can be known, but location
suggests they were among the first,
and the oldest dated stones surround them.
Perhaps, since side by side, they were siblings
who died close together in a pandemic,
or passing strangers in an accident,
or the last three of a fading family.
Obviously they were poor,
but even the poor can afford a flat
or strange stone from a creek bed.
Chances are no one was left who loved them,
for these are non-descript field stones,
abundant on the surface of this hillside
and often turned up while plowing corn
or digging even the shallowest of graves.

III. Forgotten Women in a Hill Cemetery

Nothing of them remains except names
they were given. Their people are gone,
and the family proves unfamiliar to the oldest
among us. But their names may have shaped them
as they embraced and resisted. Many were flowers—
Daisy, Lily, Violet, Rose—and were aware
their brief beauty would be plucked
and would fade. Others were blessed
or cursed with the Biblical—Sarah, Ruth,
Rebekah, Esther, Rachel, and so many Marys.
Many were precious gems—Ruby, Jewel,
Opal, Pearl—who, like the flowers,
were named for beauty, but who knew
they would have to be hard, so hard.

IV. Field of Old Farmers

They were often eager to begin the day,
to see how much could be done before dark,
and would meet the morning with tool
in hand and then hesitate to leave off
at evening. Many returned near nightfall
to survey their day's work. When they grew
too old to work, they told of their days of labor.
Others of their kind met death in the fields,
and now they all lie in this field of stones,
some in stiff, new overalls saved for the occasion,
others in their Sunday best. In many coffins
a tool was tucked away—a corn knife, hay hook,
a froe—not to be of service in an afterlife,
but because someone did not wish to see
the tool lie idle or to be tempted
to betray it into the hands of another.

V. Black Cemetery Outside of Town

The county cemetery census[1] grants
the place no name, listing it as "Negro Graves,"
and states it is "about" one-half mile south
of town and then a "short" quarter mile west
of the road in the corner of woods
"near" an open field, that it contains "maybe"
eight to ten fieldstone markers overgrown
with underbrush which "legend" says belong
to a black man "called" Art and his family,
that Art was murdered "or" died when his house
burned, and that the graves are "possibly" from
the late 1800s. All the details are uncertain.
Distance from town is uncertain, location
is uncertain, birth dates are unknown,
causes and dates of death are unknown,
names are unknown, the number of graves
is uncertain, their lives are unknown.
For this family, only death was certain.

[1] *Webster County, Missouri: Cemetery Inscriptions* by Mary Bean Cunningham, 1980, p. 62.

Amusements

"In the sun that is young once only,
Time let me play and be . . ."

Dylan Thomas
"Fern Hill"

On Her Blindness

I don't remember being aware at age four
that Mother was losing her eyesight;
my attention was captured by the grasshopper
I held prisoner in a Mason jar who kept eyes
upon escape when I inserted fresh grass;
by the bubble-eyed tadpoles I had scooped
from the creek and placed in a fish bowl;
and by how strange my name sounded when I
said it aloud with eyes closed; but I
sometimes cried on moonless nights
when darkness consumed my room.
She would come to my side and whisper,
"Don't be afraid. There's no reason to fear
the dark," but I would not be comforted.

Our Rainbow

It was summer, and I was five and you eight;
We were in the front yard playing with a wash tub
Of water, filling Mason jars and holding them
Upside down on our heads while trying to run
Around the house before they emptied.
Dad was at the mill, but that was far from us,
And Mother was working in the house.
A rare July rain had fallen that morning,
And wet grass slivers clung to our bare feet.
Our horizons were ringed with blue thunderclouds,
And as the weather folks perpetually predict,
The day was partly cloudy with scattered showers.
The sun was on us for a moment, and sprinkles
Fell somewhere. Then there were three of us
There—you, me, and the rainbow's end.
It appeared to move across our lawn; we
Pointed and dashed toward the colors, hoping
To run through them as the rainbow retreated
Ever before us and became lost in shadows
Of trees. There was no pot of gold, and we
Laughed and mocked such silly notions,
For we knew it would never be there for us.

Calling Names

When first big enough to help with milking,
I asked my older brother how cows
could know their names. He said
that they didn't really know their names
but only paired the main vowel sound
with the reward of feed. To demonstrate,
he called out the long *ō* sound, as in *go*
or *show*, and ole Jo moseyed into the barn
and slipped her head into her stanchion.
He then called out the long *ā* sound,
as in *date* or *play*, and Blaze
entered the barn and found her spot.
But when he called out the *oo* sound,
as in *choose* and *lose* Gertrude, unsure
of herself, shifted her bovine heft
from right to left, and pulled nervously
at the cuffs of her polyester blouse.

WINDYVILLE STORE

Taking Roll in Head Start: Windyville, Missouri, 1967-68

> These children will. . . . get medical and dental attention that they badly need, and parents will receive counseling on improving the home environment.
>
> President Lyndon Johnson
> Remarks on Project Head Start
> May 18, 1965

If someone was missing
when Mrs. Poole called roll,
the others shouted, "Absent!"
Absent was a mystery to me;
I had never heard the word
but was certain that it was a fun
something that others
got to do, like eating out,
going to movies, or Little League.
But one day when I was sick,
Mother said, "I bet your friends
wonder why you are absent,"
and it all made perfect sense.
I had never used the word,
had never needed the word,
for each morning and evening,
at every meal and bedtime,
Mom was always present,
Dad was always present.

When a Child, Hunting for Arrowheads

I never found one by searching,
but occasionally when at play
or fetching cows, one would flash
into sight, its intentional design
sharp against chaos of earth;
but each was always broken,
and had probably been tossed aside
like a bent nail or cracked jar,
or like a damaged forbidden tool
hidden in the dirt from Father.

Learning to Write a Poem during Art Class in First Grade at Age 56

Our art teacher, Mrs. Randall, gave
each of us one sheet of drawing paper
and told us to simply move our pencils
around without trying to draw anything
and then to color each section a different
color. She promised that if we let our hands
express our mood a picture of something
inside us would appear. I moved my pencil
around trying hard to draw nothing
and started coloring the strange shapes
and saw nothing forming on my page
or on the pages of my neighbors,
but when Lisa held hers up, Mrs. Randall
immediately saw a pony; Carl held his up,
she saw a truck; Dawn had a dog.
Knowing that I had nothing, I showed
my page, and she said, "I see a teapot!"
I knew she was humoring me, but now,
as I arrive at this line fifty years later,
I am beginning to see that teapot.

Rabbit Trap

A boy can learn a lot by building
something small, like a rabbit trap:
the difference between a curved claw
and a straight claw hammer, how to
start a nail without smashing a finger
and pull a nail without scarring the surface,
how to use a brace and bit, the variety
of saws and screws and grades
of sandpaper, how to frame a door,
the special measurements on a tape,
the capabilities of a carpenter's square,
basic geometry and physics,
the Pythagorean theorem, the use
of a fulcrum and lever, and how
to make the trigger so sensitive
that even the fleetest of foot
cannot escape the flash of darkness.

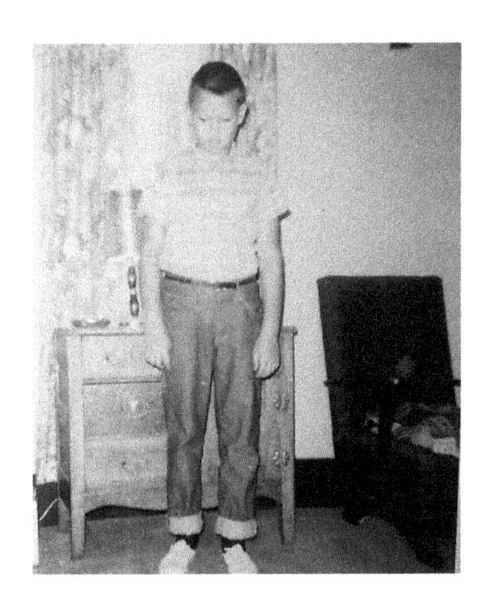

A Bluebird Fades beside an Indigo Bunting

He doesn't mind wearing faded jeans,
for he recalls the stiff dark blue denim
of those first weeks of school each year,
how his mother warned him away from games
that might damage his one new pair,
the guilt he felt when jumping out of swings
or sliding into second, how the wide,
rolled cuffs chafed his ankles,
and his parents' disappointment when
he didn't grow fast enough to unroll them.

Moon Shot, July 1969

In Mrs. Gregg's second grade we read
in our *Weekly Reader* that the astronauts
nursed tubes of turkey and drank powdered
orange juice, and at home I watched the *Eagle*
land on our black and white TV.
An elderly, illiterate neighbor man
thought that the whole project was a sin,
that the moon was the door stone of Heaven,
and that Armstrong and crew
would see straight into eternity. Dad said
no one really knew what might happen
when they touched down and that they
might just sink into the surface. I imagined
their capsule being an aluminum travel
trailer sitting on a cratered and glowing
pea-green lawn that stretched and arched
into the distance, giving way to vast blackness,
with the Earth hanging in the distance
like a drowsy blue sun.

As I fetched the cows
an hour before dawn, the lights
of the milk barn so far away,
I looked at the moon, hoping
to see a tin-foil glimmer of their ship
and felt less alone although I knew
that if they were looking down,
even through their most sophisticated
instruments, they could not see me
in these shadowed hills, wading
knee-high, dew-laden fescue
and talking to cows in the dark.

Farm Team
(Nine Innings of Senryu)

farm boy
playing baseball alone;
the barn door strikes out

he steps to the plate,
summer grasses
do the wave

a fast ball,
the barn foundation
hits another grounder

impossible catch,
witnessed by a crowd
of Holsteins

throwing to a tree,
double play
completed

a homerun!
searching for the game ball
in a neighbor's hayfield

he fouls off,
the catcher
has no chance

chore time,
the ghost runners
linger in the field

abandoned ball field,
only the wind
circles the bases

Upon Finding My Elementary Grade Cards and a Crayon Drawing in Mother's Scrapbooks

On every grade card for all those years,
her patient, graceful signature appeared
beneath a series of teachers' warnings:
"Phillip could have done better."
"Phillip turns in incomplete work."
"Phillip does not follow instructions."
"Phillip does not respond to questions."
"Phillip's work has gone down this quarter."

My indifference mystified even me,
but now, almost fifty years later,
I immediately recognize our old house,
those trees, and myself running
a foot above the ground with a smile
wider than my face under an immense sun,
and, from the chimney, a wisp
of wood smoke lingers, resisting
all the forces urging it to rise.

At Age Nine, Learning to Whistle

I tried for weeks with every breath I drew
and tortured my face and blew until blue
as I went about straining and hissing
in search of the secret I was missing.
I asked every whistler who might know,
but they said, "Pucker your lips, fool, and blow."
So I huffed and puffed, puckered and pouted,
and deflated self until I doubted
that I contained a melodious sound.
But one moment, when sad and worry bound,
out came a flat note unforced and unbidden
from some silent source where it was hidden,
and though my troubles would never be gone,
their weight was then counterbalanced by song.

Petrified Turtle

He discovered its patterned, petrified
shell half submerged in fossilized
mud or clay or tar on a late summer
day when his only companions were dry
creek bed and his dread of fourth grade.
No one bothered to believe, and gods
of the creek conjured a flood, burying
his wonder beneath gravel. Fifty years
pass, the strand shifts, and the man
who was the boy discovers it again,
but he can now only ponder if the turtle
had been trapped by the mire
or had buried itself in its dying stream.

While Cleaning the Shed

Behind clutter, leaning against the back wall,
a boat oar, one of a pair older brother shaped
from an oak board more than fifty years ago.
For two weeks that summer dad took us
early from hay fields to night fish the river,
nights of floating under and on a stream of stars,
tying limb lines, listening to the countless choir
of minute mouths, peering into silent depths,
and then falling asleep by lantern light. The boat
rotted away decades ago, the river is ruined,
but this lone oar rowed steadily on its side
of the gunwale, bending a wake through time,
until it circled back to my hands and nudged
the boat's bow upon this far bank of memory.

Distant Train

> The Laclede and Ft. Scott Railroad "was never built. . . . Today there is not an inch of railroad in Dallas County."
>
> Anna O'Brien
> "Place Names of Five Central
> Southern Counties of Missouri."

On dark and bare winter mornings
while bringing cows to barn
I sometimes heard, coming up
the creek valley, the faint rumble
and whistle of a train eight miles
away in a neighboring county.
My elementary friends scoffed,
knowing no track entered our hills,
but they could not imagine the stillness
of those early hours, the long windings
of the valley, or how darkness collapses
distance. Their dismissal forestalled
obvious metaphors of movement
and adventure and escape, and I knew
it was already too late for many of them.

The Call

> Many examples of Scots-Irish usage prevail to this day [. . . .] *Sook*, *Sookie*, or *Sook Cow* is the local cry farmers use to summon the herd and comes from the Old English sūcan meaning "to suck."
>
> *The Story of English*
> Robert McCrum
> William Cran
> Robert MacNeil

After washing away a day of sweat
and sawdust earned at the mill,
Dad would eat supper and then call
to his milk cows as he walked
from house to barn, "Sook, Sook,
Come on," unaware that this word
was an ancient call of Scots-Irish
husbandmen, but the cows recognized
the call, raised heads, and called back
with voices and udders swelling.

The Farm Youth's Companion

Death was in the cemetery of strangely named ancestors,
in old farmers with abandoned cancers on their faces,
in the family that slept through a flue fire on the first cold night of fall,
in the bloated circle of cows rounding a lightning-struck black oak,
in the ancient, shrunken great-uncle on his deathbed spitting tobacco juice
    and blood,
in the little goats poisoned by spring grasses,
in the classmate who fell from a tractor and into his father's machine,
in the hound lost in a scent crossing a busy road,
in the remains of an old woman burning leaves alone in a long dress,
in the bullhead and bluegill minnows gulping at surface air in the last
    muddy puddle spared by drought,
in the blind boy who panicked while swimming and drowned his brother
    with him,
in the framed photographs of farm boys stiff in new uniforms,
in the lamb that could not nurse,
in every Sunday's soundings of vengeance and brimstone,
in young wrens and their mother swallowed into a blacksnake's darker
    night,
in the gutted deer hanging by hushed heels,
in the reclusive widow not missed for more than a month,
in the frantic, defiant cries of coyotes,
in the stillborn calf licked clean by its mother,
in prophecies of whippoorwills,
in the broken farmer hanging from a rafter.

It waited in the cottonmouth lying in the limbs over-hanging the
    swimming hole,
in the undercurrents of the flooded stream,
in the falling of a log tree,
in the rock or stob pitched by the brush hog,
in the inviting silence of the thinly frozen pond,
in the rotted floorboards of the high hay loft,
in the nest of red wasps in the corner of the machine shed,
in the spinning whispers of the power shaft,
in the science of stagnant waters,
in the screaming jealous jaws of the mother sow,
in the hunger of the wood saw,

in the cracked rung of a ladder,
in the kick of a horse or mule,
in the hay dust stored for seasons in the lung,
in the proud bull in the pasture,
in the decayed rails of the tree house,
in the depths of the hand-dug well,
in the avalanche of hay bales,
in the poisoned rust of a nail,
in the airy and comforting whirl of the mill blade.

Death was dealt to the bait in the bucket,
to the fish quivering under the blade,
to the pet steer called to slaughter by the rattle of his feed pail,
to the sack of unwanted kittens,
to an old dog led the last time to woods,
to young rabbits and mice in the freshly mown field,
to the possum in the trap,
to the water snake sunning in warm sand,
to the sinewy squirrel stripped of his skin,
to the racoon in the tree,
to the frog impaled and gesticulating on the gig,
to the quail in their flush of rising,
to the chicken on the block blinking as the hatchet fell cross the sun,
to the headless, croaking chickens tossed into tall grasses to bleed and
settle,
to the gentle, worn-out milk cow sold to market,
to the fattened hog lifting his face to the rifle, smiling.

Her Wheelbarrow

It was originally deep teal,
but after years of use,
she painted it barn red,
and much later, butter yellow.

Her paints are peeling,
revealing the colors beneath,
looking much like a map
of a shrinking empire.

With each season the teal,
tranquil seas encroach
ever more upon the red
realms she once possessed
and drown the soft glow
of lands she dared not explore.

At Her Woodpile

at her woodpile,
old widow counting the sticks
needed to reach spring

New Garden in an Abandoned Horse Corral

The soil is rich here
from years of composted manure,
and my plants grow
restless, animated.

Sweet potato vines,
with their trailing instinct
roam among the rows.

Tomatoes, their lithe limbs
trained inside wire cages,
grow heavy with foal.

Pole beans loiter
along the high fence
and hang their heads
over to sway in the air.

Corn stalks knicker
as the breeze rises
and nuzzle my shoulder
as I weed and water.

And they all watch,
as though waiting for me,
lulled by summer air,
to leave the gate ajar.

Hidden

In the new moon midnight
he climbed the tallest tree
in the deepest woods,
stole the blackest feather
from a crow deep in sleep,

gathered blackberries
from shadowed vines,
boiled their juices
in a black pot
over a hidden fire,

dipped the black feather
into the black broth,
and wrote a name backwards
in the blackest cavern
at midnight with eyes closed.

In random blackness
he crawls backwards
into the depths of the cave
to touch her name
with fingers gloved
in darkness.

Ancient Cedar

ancient cedar tree,
broken, bare, useless—until
this moon rose in it

Displacements

"O'er ruined fences the grape-vines shield
The woods come back to the mowing field."

Robert Frost
"Ghost House"

The Redbuds

> "O, let me not be mad, not mad, sweet heaven!"
> King Lear

Surely we tolerate and cultivate them
for more than their brief purple beauty,
for they fade into shade of taller trees
and shadows of their heavy heart-like leaves,
where they spend the remainder of time
harming themselves, twisting and torturing
their trunks, ranging limbs out in impossible
angles as though begging wind and ice
to break them, and they grow mad and gray,
shed shingles of thinning bark, go hollow,
and we find them in early spring
where they have thrown themselves prone,
exhausted and spent in their despair,
and we prop them up with a cinder block
or cord wood as they remind us of what we
must not allow ourselves to do or be.

Century Farm

I. The Folklorist

I stopped to ask an Ozarks farmer about
the house at the end of his dead-end road
and who had lived there and where they had gone.
It stood without paint and no flowers framed
its fenceless lawn, and the rock foundation
was sinking unevenly into the ground.

"I bought that place from the probate court.
The family all died or moved away;
no one by that name around here no more.

"The grandmother moved them here from the South
during the Civil War after the loss
of a husband and a son. The family
then farmed that ground for three generations.
They built a cabin where the house now stands;
in 1910 they rolled it with logs and ox
to leave only the sandstone chimney
to build the balloon-frame house against.

"The last of them was Everett, a bachelor,
and his sister. He promised his mother
he would not marry while the girl lived,
and she lived until he was an old man—
too old to marry and begin a life.
He locked her upstairs when he rode to town
or to teach school, and she often locked
herself away when company came to call
and paced above to worry them away.
He didn't do it out of meanness, no;
he always tried to do the best by her
and gave her a bed, a chair, picture books,
and lace curtains—nothing to harm herself.

"When she died, I helped Everett bury her
beside their mother, and when he died,

us neighbors buried him beside their dad.
That was the end; that is, it should have been,
but renters came to occupy the house,
though none of them stayed long, just long enough
to find another place.

"A loneliness
is there, a wish, perhaps, for what should be.
Sometimes I sense her watching from her room
as she often watched there for his return.
Smile if you want, but I hire a boy
to work with me when I work near the house.
She seemed to be a soul that didn't know
that it was here, so her soul may not know
that she is now supposed to be gone.
I tell myself it must be wind that lifts
away the yellowed lace from the window,
but I got no interest in proving that."

He gave me a key to let myself in,
and another for the stairway lock.
A hook-and-eye held the outside of her door.
The room was unfinished tongue-and-groove pine.
The three windows were nailed shut but held views
of rolling hills and a winding dirt road.
All had been sold at auction years before
except a bookshelf made from an apple crate,
a stack of *Life*, and a straw mattress bound
in rough white cotton cloth of feed sacks.
I had intended to photograph the house,
but it had lost its charm, and I had lost
my foolish notion of wanting walls to talk.

II. Mother Jane

In the Family Cemetery

I wanted my two girls to marry well—
not suffer the worry that was my life
as a wife and widow with four children.
My husband died when Rose, a late last child,
was three. He commanded that the farm stay
in the family and the family
remain on the farm. Everett, the son,
had the job of carrying on. The girls
could not marry if forced to care for Rose,
or if the eligible men were shown
the madness that inhabited our blood.

Rose was comfortable with Everett.
He was a man when she became aware
of him, so any change in him was slow.
Her sisters, though, blossomed into women
before her troubled eyes and upset her
because she could sense in them what she would
never become. For her good, they needed
to marry themselves away from this farm.
They did. Both married up and into town
and had all the nicer things I never.
They did their duty, and I stayed to do
mine as long as I was able. Rose came
so late in life, and I was old when she
was no more than a girl.

Everett did
his duty. I never asked him, never
demanded it of him. I recognized
his sacrifice and told him how good he
was to look after Rose once I was gone.
He promised not to marry, for he knew
Rose would know no peace but at home away
from all others and among her own things.
I didn't demand it of him, not once,
for he was brought up knowing what is right.

III. Sister Rose

Beside the Mother

I am now, of course, able to see all—
the madness and fear, sacrifice and guilt—
that filled the shadows that haunted my life.
Nothing can be seen complete until it
is past, and while living, nothing is ever past,
ever complete, for in every moment
something new begins—the sounds and smells
and movements of any moment do not cease
to let others begin, and all blend into
meanings and moods that could not be said
and that no one but me seemed to sense.

Fear was in the eyes of my sisters; not fear
of not understanding me, but fear of becoming me.
They would rush out when their men came to call
and meet them before they could enter the lawn gate,
and mother quickly stepped out on the porch
to greet them and tell them goodbye in one breath.
I was their curse, yet Mama cared for me;
that is, she cared for the person she thought
I should have been and the one she prayed
that I might yet be. Her guilt shone around her
like the morning sun in the white curtains
of my east window.
Everett understood.
He always let me know I was. He talked
to me by talking to himself—self talk
is the most honest talk—and let me
into himself without my needing to answer.
He did so many quiet things for me.
He polished my shoes, let kitty into
my room each morning, built snowmen
outside my window to wave at me,
and left each crusty corner piece of cake.

While alive, I had one moment of clarity,
but it was a dream. We were in our wagon,

and Everett was driving the horses.
I had never been to town and was excited.
The road was muddy and rutted from rain,
but Everett assured us we could get to town.
But Jones Creek was flooding, so Everett
had to turn the horses to take the higher road,
and he kept driving farther from town.
One by one my mother and sisters stood
and shouted wild and wordless ravings,
like March winds wailing through an empty barn.
They ignored each other. I turned laughing
to Everett but saw that he was wrapped from neck
to feet in burlap and tied with thick rope.
For that one moment I realized they
were angry and miserable and that my
madness was destroying my family.
I wanted to release them, to tell them
to put me away and enjoy their lives,
but that thought faded into my nightmare.

The Quarry

The rolling hills and milk cows
never made the grandfather
or the father rich, but the son
was determined to make the farm pay
at any cost. He saw thin dirt
as an obstacle to his fortune
and sold topsoil to blast limestone.
He soon made fools of the old folks
by turning rock into gold. The newspaper
visited but couldn't mine enough superlatives
out of the English language to express
the benefits and beauty the Chamber
of Commerce saw in his operation.
He related for readers again the story
of how the family had toiled
and of how only he had succeeded.
But the people he speaks for are gone,
as is their place of struggle and life,
and gravel trucks circle like buzzards
as they spread the farm to build
the new four-lane north of town.

Homestead on the Buffalo National River

> The Buffalo National River became America's first national river when President Richard Nixon signed Public Law 92-237 on March 1, 1972.

Everything about this place says,
Stay here. Seek no further.
All is crafted to provide wealth
of contentment for generations
beyond the builders: the welcoming
slam of the wooden screen door,
the dove-tail joints, the massive
fireplace stones, the southern sun
falling upon the cupboard,
the snug laying boxes in the hen house,
the protective overhang of the barn roof.
Most visitors, even those well
beyond the age of starting anew,
who stop for a moment on their way
to somewhere else, camera dangling
and car idling, feel this urge.
This pioneer family did stay
for more than 150 years,
and it took an Act of Congress
to make them leave.

When the Milk Cans Became Unemployed

Some found positions with the postal service
holding rural mailboxes, pleased to have landed
federal jobs; others found seasonal work
hauling water during drought; a few

accepted reduced positions in the dairy business
transporting soured milk to hungry hogs;
others submitted to retirement and loiter
around the farm with their metal caps

cocked in mock independence; some
moved to town with their elderly bosses
and stand on either side of the porch
with "Welcome" painted on their bellies

and sporting geraniums; others
found part-time work holding umbrellas
and walking canes at the café or cigarette
butts in front of the laundromat; several,

unable to learn a new skill, stand
with the other displaced collectibles
outside flea markets, waiting
for someone to invent a use for them.

Lost

Outside the flea market
an old milk can,
confused by rust and emptiness,
raises its little arms to me
like a lost toddler.

Barn Swallows

> But the quiet places . . . in this part of the country
> are getting fewer and smaller.
>
> Edsel Ford (Arkansas Poet)
> *The Ozarks Mountaineer*
> July 1966

The parent birds flitted
　　　　hundreds of times
through the upper corner
　　　　of the barn door
with mouths full
　　　　of mud and grass
while we milked below.

Each trip seemed
　　　　synchronized
to the blinking
　　　　of the human eye
until the birds
　　　　became as invisible
as the blink of an eye.

They built adobe
　　　　nests in raftered silence,
seeking only to live
　　　　and to raise their brood
in that high,
　　　　shadowed perch.

Persimmon Tree at Leyda and Summit

I passed by several mornings
without recognizing her,
for she appears to be a cultivated
shade tree, having shaped herself
to fill a place in the lawn
and no longer hemmed in
by a grove of kinfolk who remain
back home feeding possums
and raccoons, boiling bitter jelly,
and splitting their seeds
to predict winter. But now
when meeting early mornings,
before the city people are awake
and watching, we greet
one another, discuss the weather,
study the gathering clouds,
listen for calls of a rain crow,
and avoid any mention of home.

Barn Removal

The barn swallows return again
by instinct, following a homing device
to this place where a barn stood
for more than a century.
Torn down during winter,
only its foundation remains,
ruins beyond the birds' reckoning,
and they dive and circle,
almost losing grace to confusion,
and then they alight on a power wire
and tap their instrument panels.

Journal Entry: May 13, 2018

Young mulberries hold their birth fuzz
as kittens, five weeks old, discover irises.
Hay grasses grow heavy headed,
and whirligigs whirl in green breezes.
The wet-weather creek gurgles, roils with spring.

Soon the berries will ripen and will fall,
staining the walk with seeded, purple juice.
The hay will be cut and baled, the fields bare,
the creek will stand in silent, dying pools,
and a stranger will pull off the highway
to inquire about a free kitten.

Settlers' Cabin

The brothers arrived in 1836
and built a one-room cabin
of virgin white oak near the creek,
and they built it to last with dove-tail
notches and a fireplace of the largest
stones that they and their mule
could pull up the slope a quarter mile
to their place; the next generation
added a kitchen and pantry on the south;
and the next built two bedrooms
on the east made of sawmill lumber;
the fourth generation tacked up
some genuine veneer paneling
to cover the embarrassment of logs
and pulled in electricity for more light
and sound; and the next generation
added running water and an indoor
toilet and covered all this in country-blue
vinyl siding; and the last generation
moved to town.

Groundhogs: A Parable

> So profound is this sleep that even if the animal
> is warmed up, it requires several hours to awaken.
> *The Wild Mammals of Missouri*
> Charles W. and Elizabeth R. Schwartz

They were born and raised in the barn;
its arching loft roof was their sky,
the knotholes and cracks in the walls
the sounds of their winds, a century
of feed dust and hay dust the soils
of their burrows, but after the man died,
the barn began a slow fall, and his wife
hired it removed. With this local
structure gone, they were not shielded
from the larger world, and their sun
became hotter, their winters colder,
and flooding of their homes common.
Several had to move away, taking
up residence under an abandoned truck,
in the garbage dump, under the chicken
coop, and even beneath her house.
Some of them were reduced to petty
thievery, stealing her tomatoes
and stripping young leaves from sweet
potato vines, and she began setting traps,
and though warned not to play near
these wire cages, many of the young
could not resist the sweet odors
of apple slices and peanut butter.
Now the old ones weary themselves
trying to whistle away their worries,
and even in winter, when they should
be wrapped in death-like sleep, they wake
one another, and she hears them pacing
and murmuring under the floorboards
and silently joins them in fretting about
what will become of the grandchildren.

She Recalls Moving to this Farm Sixty Years Ago

> From a northeast-to-southwest line near the center
> of the [Ozarks] dome, the drainage runs northward
> to the Osage, Gasconade, Meramec, and Missouri
> rivers and southward to the White, Eleven Point,
> Current, Black, and St. Francis rivers.
>
> Milton D. Rafferty
> *The Ozarks: Land and Life*

This creek always ran the wrong direction,
but I loved his farm, this house, barn, and hill.
So flow the deep currents of affection.

It prompted a childhood recollection
every time I waded its backward rill.
This creek always ran the wrong direction.

To this county I had no connection.
Following my husband became my will.
So flow the deep currents of affection.

To leave my home place was a concession,
and after sixty years, I miss it still.
This creek always ran the wrong direction.

Sometimes, when his brooding begged correction,
I'd allude to my loss with woman's skill.
So flow the deep currents of affection.

Its contrary course was my resurrection,
reminding me of myself to fulfill.
This creek always ran the wrong direction.
So flow the deep currents of affection.

Prickly Pear

It should be far southwest of these hills;
an oddity here, it must have thrown itself
flat among the rocks as glaciers retreated
to avoid being dragged away. It maintains
that instinct and presses itself to the ground
each winter and deflates and darkens
and wrinkles its pads, and, like a woodchuck,
slows its pulse and drops its body temperature
and with needled fingers clutches cast-off leaves
like an old widow clutching a faded scarf.
But in spring it rises from its leaf bed,
arching its arms, a living Stonehenge,
cupping each passing sun and pressing
that warmth into brilliant yellow blossoms,
each melting away after one day,
and then it spends the rest of summer
taking one cat-like step due south.

A Fence in Woods

A rusted woven wire fence
topped with a strand of barbed
runs through this rocky, dry ridge
of timber, and a hand-dug pond
deep in the woods holds a puddle
during wet seasons. Someone
may have tried to raise hogs here,
hoping to fatten them on acorns, roots,
and copperheads, but now that fence
rises and falls, occasionally rearing
from leaf fodder to where it has grown
into the thin rings of a blackjack oak,
and then falling again into leaf bed,
much like these hills rise and fall
until they lie quiet in a prairie
or plain, or like this farm rose
and fell with hope and despair
until it failed, or like a family name
that struggled to rise until it left
this place or was buried under it.

Peele's Barn

Old Man Peele was a master carpenter,
and he laid the entire barn out in the grass
before neighbors arrived to raise it.
No nails were needed in the frame,
which he had hewed from white oaks,
for every joint and juncture, every mortise
and tenon met and matched as he had foreseen.
He had known all that would need to be done
and when and in what order. It was raised
in two days, six were not needed, and it
was built so well that it outlived the old man
and his family, and outlived the mode of life
and farm that produced it. Now only a poet
or folklorist is found foolish enough to trust
its loft ladder and loft floor and to peer
through its cracks at the lost world outside.

Wallpaper in the Abandoned House

It is torn and peeling, revealing
layer upon layer of older paper,
like rings of a tree stunted in poor soil,
and each offers a different design—
paisley, geometrics, various florals—
and they probably re-arranged
the furniture and turned the rug
with each papering, but the new
was soon yellowed and stained
by the same woodsmoke, the same
fried fat back, his cigarettes;
and, like their thin imagination,
the paper covered the walls,
but could never make them go away.

Turkey Buzzards

Throughout summer they roosted
in a dead oak on my neighbor's
back acreage, and now in November
their relations flock in, congregating,
contemplating a move farther south.
Their sleeping quarters and coasting
circles grow crowded, yet they hesitate
to leave town—perhaps the rent
is paid up to the end of the month,
or they are waiting for Uncle Baldy's
brood to glide in. Most likely,
this lingering warm weather
and their rare avian sense of smell
has convinced them that the season
of death has not ended, and I
see them each morning perched
on bare limbs, their dreaded red
and raw faces facing first rays,
and, since granted no voice to sing,
they hold wings half raised, accepting
with silent grace the grace given.

Dirt, Tree, Sky

She visits the old home place her last time.
This year she has to return by herself,
for no one else remains who remembers.
She hardly recognizes where to turn—
the road has been widened and straightened,
and the mailbox is now flanked on both sides
by recent boxes and names. The driveway
is shorter, a dust is on everything.
Even before parking, she sees the loft barn
is gone. Only its foundation remains,
and it appears far too small for the worlds
once there. A garage fills the garden plot.
All the fence lines have moved, and the calf lot
and chicken pen have faded into lawn.
The hill has shrunken, and the horizons
rise and fall with strange rhythms. She becomes
dizzy and short of breath and uncertain
of where she parked and begins to wish she
had not come. She sees the mulberry tree,
the one her mother always said had been
"dying for a hundred years," and she leans
against its gray and flaking bark and bows
her head to catch her breath and to focus
upon the earth at her feet. She recalls
playing in this dirt as a child, recalls
climbing on the low, crippled limb above.
Raising her eyes, she sees the limb still there,
its elbow still pointing due north, and now
shadows of the old farm fall into place,
and she remembers who she was, who she
became, and how to find her way back home.

Mother Thinned Marigolds in July and Gave Me Some to Transplant

They moved in from two counties over
during the height of drought.
They didn't know anyone around here,
and being uprooted and sun scorched,
they grew weak and withdrawn
until late summer showers stirred
their spirits. Although they now work
to keep pests from tomatoes and beans,
they dress flashy, causing the sober potatoes,
who will soon face the shovel themselves,
to complain in flat and starchy tones
about what is happening to the neighborhood.

Essays

"Nothing now is left but a Majestic memory."

Henry Wadsworth Longfellow
"Three Friends of Mine"

Four Mile Creek

As children, most of us had a special place to play. In these corners of our world, we acted out our constructions of life, exercised our imaginations, and formed memories that made us who we are. I was lucky, for I had miles of hills and hollers to roam. I also had a creek, the crown jewel of amusements.

My mother still lives on the farm where I was raised. It is a typical Ozarks farm—a little pasture, a couple of hills, some rocks and trees, and the creek bending through its middle. The house sits on one of the hills, and the room where I slept as a child faces south and looks down the slope at the creek.

When I stay overnight, my first act in the morning is the same as when I was a boy—I glance out the window at the creek. Such an odd act. Perhaps the creek was an assurance of reality, for it was always there regardless of how unreliable the rest of the world became. Maybe it was a natural guide to my fortunes for the day, for some mornings it would be running clear, reflecting stars and moon, and other mornings it would be slow and stagnant, burdened with the gloom of clouds.

My older brother, Tom, and I had a rock collection, and most of our gems were mined from the creek. We had chalk rocks, sand rocks, and sparkly rocks. We had rocks that looked like marbles or peanuts or cavemen's teeth. Once, when we had acquired a surplus, we decided to offer a limited selection to the public. There was a small, leaning chicken house on the side of the hill west of our house, and we opened shop there. Our inventory cost us nothing, and each flooding of the creek brought a new supply. We had low overhead, so we could sell our wares at rock-bottom prices and get rich quick. The only customers to enter our secluded shop were some red wasps and a blacksnake, but no one, except some children, would have recognized the value of our stones.

We sometimes had a water gate where Four Mile Creek exited the farm. With each flood, the gate would be washed away. One rainy evening, when I went to fetch the cows, there were no cows, for they had discovered the absence of the gate and had ventured downstream to a neighbor's woods a mile away. When we found them, they were scattered and running through the woods like children in a new playground, hurrying from the swing set to the sliding board to the sandbox to the merry-go-round, astonished at this world just beyond their fences. However, too much freedom can be terrifying, and after their initial frolic they wished to be herded home.

During the wet seasons, Four Mile would often flood during the night, and the next morning the cows would be on the opposite bank from the milk barn. Tom and I would walk down the gravel road that bordered the east side of the farm, wade across the flooded low-water bridge, crawl through the fence, and herd the cows to the barn. They would hesitate before entering the rolling waters, yet, cattle, like sheep and people, are mobbish, and if one of them does something, the rest are more willing to try. They would wade into the current, swim while floating downstream a few rods, and bobble out on the far bank. Almost any being can swim if it has to, and after you have seen a cow swim, you will believe most anything is possible.

My best friend in elementary school lived on a farm a few miles downstream. One day, at high tide, I decided to send him a message in a bottle. These were the days before plastic soda pop bottles, so finding a bottle with a tight-fitting lid was difficult. Glass pop bottles were transparent gold—worth a nickel each. I didn't dare steal one of my mother's canning jars. I found an odd little bottle, one like cooking vanilla or shoe polish was sold in, but it didn't have a lid. I whittled a stick to plug the hole, wrote my message, and tossed my communiqué in the water. I ran along the bank to watch my vessel begin its voyage. It lodged in a small log jam. The seal around my wooden cork was not up to specifications, and the bottle began taking on water. I couldn't reach it with a stick, so I threw some rocks to splash it loose. One rock fell too close, and my message disappeared into the murky water. Effective communication is a difficult art.

Between early spring and full summer, Four Mile would change from a torrent of muddy water to a clear stream teeming with frogs and minnows and crawdads and water striders. By midsummer the creek would undergo another metamorphosis. The gravel and rocks where the ripples had run would become plastered with the cardboard-like residue of former waters. The pools where I'd waded and splashed just weeks before were reduced to lukewarm, green puddles trampled by cattle seeking coolness and relief from heel flies. This remaining water was filled with a myriad of tadpoles, infant bullhead catfish, and tiny bluegills suffocating from lack of oxygen. Thousands hatched to die in the sun, and this drama was played every summer. One July day, Tom and I filled two ten-gallon milk cans with these legions, and we rode with Dad to pour them into the Niangua River. Days later, the remainder of the water had dried away, and there remained no clue, except the sun-bleached pinchers of crawfish, that life had ever existed in Four Mile.

At different times we tried to build a dam to create a swimming hole, tried to build a raft with milk cans, were chased out of our wading hole by a cottonmouth, and had many other mishaps and adventures along the creek. It was the center of my play and imagination, and all its moods were reflected through me. The creek is still there, but it is diminished. Perhaps it's only childhood imagination that allows me to believe there was once enough water to float a raft, or that its waters were once clean enough to drink, or that it once offered life and mystery.

Off the Farm

In the summer of 1972, when I was ten years old, my dad sold a crop of wheat to a feed mill in Springfield, Missouri, fifty miles from our farm. He harvested the crop with an ancient Allis-Chalmers combine, bagged the grain in burlap sacks, and stacked it on our old farm truck to haul to market.

We did our weekly shopping in towns much closer to home, and this longer trip was a special occasion and required planning. My parents made a list of items that could be purchased only in the larger town—chainsaw parts, sewing machine needles, replacement teeth for our sawmill blade—and a list of places my mother wanted to shop. We seldom traveled so far from home, and the truck rarely left the farm, so this trip was certain to be a great adventure.

Although the trip was to be made in a dilapidated work truck loaded with grain, the entire family would be going, for no one wanted to miss such rare fun. On such trips, my older brother, Tom, and I followed Dad to pawn shops to peruse the hand tools and hunting rifles, and we would sometimes join Mom at the Goodwill store to try on clothing and browse the used toys. Our last stop was usually a discount bakery where Tom and I would buy a sack of eight-for-a-dollar pastries to eat on the long drive home.

Our truck was a 1951 Chevrolet two-ton flatbed. On the underside of its fenders and doors some of its original dark blue paint remained, which, on hot summer days in the dry hayfields reminded me of shaded pools of water along Duesenberry Creek. The rest of the truck's metal had faded to a weathered and rusted brown. It was a big truck, but it had a small six-cylinder engine. The Chevy six cylinders were the workhorses of American highways before the highways became an interstate system filled with screaming diesel trucks. Our truck had enough power and speed to haul hay from field to barn or to haul logs from woods to mill, but on the modern roads, the rest of the world quickly passed it by.

Tom and I spent the summer hauling hay, cutting brush, working cattle, and building fence. We were chigger bitten and briar scratched, lean and hard as fence posts, and brown as ticks, and sported practical haircuts and practical clothing. Dad had a pair of Sears Roebuck electric clippers, and he knew how to give a buzz cut. Mom made many of our shirts, often making them match for school photos. So, on the morning of our Springfield expedition, my dad, mom, and two-year-old brother sat in the cab of the truck, and Tom and I climbed on top of the sacked grain and sat there in our matching red-and-white checkered shirts, chigger bites, farm tans, and buzz cuts, thrilled to be taking a cool and breezy ride to town.

The truck was notorious for mechanical failures, such as a dead battery, fouled spark plugs, a leaking and overheating radiator, or flooding carburetor;

but on that day, it was running like a new sewing machine, rolling down the highway with its tires humming a contented song of the open road. It seemed to be enjoying the day off the farm as much as I was—happy to get out and see the world and to blow the field dust off its wheels.

We always enjoyed riding in the back of the truck. It was great fun, especially in summer, to stand in the back and let the wind blow around us, to tease the dogs that ran out to bark, and to grab at the branches and leaves hanging over the gravel roads. The only bad experience I ever had while riding in the back was when a June bug hit me between the eyes at fifty miles per hour. I was stunned for a moment, but then I wiped the bug's remains off with my shirttail. But on this trip, all the world was well. Although there were no dogs to tease and no leaves to grab, the sun was shining, the air was cool, I had a dollar in my pocket, and we were seeing the sights of a highway we seldom traveled—Interstate 44.

Near the midpoint of our trip stood Northview Hill. Northview is a steep and curving grade of more than a mile on the interstate west of Marshfield, and the truck immediately sensed this incline, and as we continued up the hill, it slowed and slowed until it found a pace it could maintain. Everything with wheels was passing us as though we were a billboard. Near the top, a brown van pulled into the passing lane and then slowed to our speed as it drew beside us. At first, I thought that these folks, like us, were having difficulty pulling the hill. After a few moments of curiosity, I glanced at the van; a woman passenger had rolled her window down and was smiling at me. Thinking that she must be someone who knew us, I stared intently at her face trying to recognize her. At that moment, she lifted a camera and snapped our picture, then snapped another. Laughing, she rolled up her window, turned to the driver, and the van sped away.

Tom was only three years older than I, but, being the oldest son on a farm, he had grown up fast, and he always seemed to have understanding beyond his years. He, too, had seen the woman and was looking at her when she took the first photo. He became quiet and sat still, facing the wind, staring at the point on the horizon where the road met the sky and ignored my questions. I was puzzled. Why would a stranger want a photo of us? I crawled to the front of the load and yelled the story to my mother through her open window. She laughed a knowing laugh that only puzzled me further.

I can't recall the rest of the day. I don't remember unloading the grain. I don't remember eating my dollar's worth of doughnuts and pies and brownies and cupcakes. It is as though my mind spent the day outside my body curiously studying its curious owner. I do recall that I did not stand to face the wind on the way home, but, instead, sat on the floor hidden by the wooden grain racks. What the woman thought she saw, I gradually realized over the years. I would love to have a copy of that photograph.

About the Author

Phillip Howerton, a sixth generation Ozarker, was brought up on a small farm in southern Dallas County, Missouri. After spending several years as a milk truck driver, a production worker, and a beef farmer, he earned degrees in English, history, and education from Drury University and a doctorate in English from the University of Missouri-Columbia. He has taught English at colleges and universities in the Ozarks for more than twenty years, is co-founder and co-editor of *Cave Region Review* and general editor of *Elder Mountain: A Journal of Ozarks Studies*, and his essays, reviews, and poems have appeared in a wide variety of journals. His poetry collection, *The History of Tree Roots*, was published by Golden Antelope Press in 2015, and his anthology, *The Literature of the Ozarks*, was published by University of Arkansas Press in 2019. He received the 2019 Missouri Literary Award from the Missouri Library Association.

Passing

Let it come on a late June evening
When whippoorwills chant
In twilight between woods and pasture,
As the moon sets near the porch
Where the dog stretches into sleep
And cats chase night shadows,
When winds rest and curtains
Hold themselves motionless,
Long after evening chores
Are done, and as mothers call
Their children in from dusty play.